PEACHTREE CITY LIBRARY
201 Willowbend Road
Peachtree, GA 30269

SPORTS STARS

GREG MADDUX

PITCHING ACE

By Ted Cox

CHILDRENS PRESS®
CHICAGO

Photo Credits

Cover, 5, ©Scott Cunningham/Sportschrome East/West; 6, Reuters/Bettmann; 9, ©Don Smith/Sports Photo Masters, Inc.; 10, ©Jonathan Daniel/Allsport USA; 13 (top), 14, UPI/Bettmann; 13 (bottom), Allsport USA; 17, ©The Des Moines Register; 19, ©Jonathan Kirn/Sports Photo Masters, Inc.; 20, AP/Wide World; 23, 24, UPI/Bettmann; 27 (top), ©Jonathan Kirn/Sports Photo Masters, Inc.; 27 (bottom), Focus on Sports; 28, AP/Wide World; 30, ©Jerry Wachter/Focus on Sports; 31, Reuters/Bettmann; 32, AP/Wide World; 33, ©Stephen Green/Allsport USA; 34, AP/Wide World; 35, 37 (all three photos), Reuters/Bettmann; 38, AP/Wide World; 41, ©Jonathan Kirn/Sports Photo Masters, Inc.; 42, ©Scott Cunningham/Sportschrome; 46, 47, Reuters/Bettmann

Staff

Project Editor: Mark Friedman
Design: Herman Adler Design Group
Photo Editor: Jan Izzo

Library of Congress Cataloging-in-Publication Data

Cox, Ted
Greg Maddux : pitching ace / by Ted Cox.
p. cm. – (Sports stars)
ISBN 0-516-04389-7
1. Maddux, Greg, 1966– —Juvenile literature. 2. Baseball players—United States—Biography—Juvenile literature. 3. Pitchers (Baseball)—United States—Biography—Juvenile literature. [1. Maddux, Greg, 1966– . 2. Baseball players.] I. Title. II. Title: Pitching ace. III. Series.
GV865.M233C69 1995
796.357'092—dc20 94-36915
[B] CIP
AC

Printed in the United States of America.
1 2 3 4 5 6 7 8 9 10 R 04 03 02 01 00 99 98 97 96 95

GREG MADDUX

PITCHING ACE

☆ ☆ ☆

Greg Maddux has always surprised people. He doesn't look much like a star athlete. He is of average height at six feet tall, and he has a boyish face. Don Zimmer, one of his old managers, had a nickname for him—"The Kid."

But his teammates know better. They know that on the pitcher's mound, Greg is a tough competitor. He doesn't have a blazing fastball. While some aces like Randy Johnson can throw the ball 100 miles per hour, Greg Maddux throws only in the mid-80s. But Greg is what's known as "sneaky fast." One of his catchers, Joe Girardi, says his fastball "explodes" as it nears home plate. Maddux can put a tail on his fastball or throw it to sink. He also throws a curve, a slider, and one of the best change-ups in baseball. Greg knows how to pitch, how to change speeds, and how to keep his pitches on the corners.

☆ ☆ ☆

"He can throw the ball wherever he wants, spots his fastball and all his pitches," says Steve Avery, a fellow pitcher on the Atlanta Braves. "He mixes speeds so well, he just keeps guys off balance."

Most of all, Greg knows how to win. Over a seven-year period (1988–94), he won more games than any other pitcher in the majors—123. Chicago sportswriter Bob Verdi once called him "a baby-faced assassin." Greg's teammates have a nickname for him, too—"Mad Dog."

There is a lot more to Greg's personality than just his attitude on the field. He has a wife, Kathy, and a daughter, Amanda Paige. They have homes in Atlanta and in his boyhood hometown, Las Vegas. Greg plays Nintendo, and he likes TV sitcoms like "The Simpsons," "Seinfeld," and "Roseanne," as well as National Geographic animal specials. He likes to listen to Garth Brooks. He is soft-spoken in interviews, but a prankster in the clubhouse.

Greg is an intense competitor on the mound, but off the field, he is quiet and soft-spoken.

Greg began earning the respect of his teammates in his early days with the Chicago Cubs.

☆ ☆ ☆

All of this can surprise people when Greg takes the mound. He is an intense competitor. Greg's intensity and skill have made him the best pitcher in baseball. He is a three-time winner of the National League Cy Young Award. Says former teammate Andre Dawson, "Greg Maddux? I'll play behind him any time."

Gregory Alan Maddux was born on April 14, 1966, in San Angelo, Texas, the youngest son of Dave and Linda Maddux. Dave was in the Air Force, so he was assigned to many different bases around the world. The Maddux family even lived in Spain at one time. Wherever the family lived, Greg and his older brother, Mike, played baseball.

☆ ☆ ☆

Greg's favorite player was Pete Rose. Greg and Mike would pitch against one another and pretend they were facing Rose and his Cincinnati Reds. Mike was almost five years older than Greg, but Mike says, "We would do things to even it out. In baseball, I would hit from the backstop, he would hit from second base. When we played basketball, I would play on my knees."

Greg didn't need help like that for long. He was never big for his age, but he was a natural athlete. "I always knew Greg was something special," says his father. "He always played in levels above his age. When Mike was 11, his friends would ask Greg to play, too, and that told me something."

As a boy, Greg idolized the great hitter, Pete Rose (top), who collected more hits than any other player in history. Greg (left) is now considered one of the best hitting pitchers in baseball.

CUBS
PONY

☆ ☆ ☆

The Maddux family settled down in Las Vegas, Nevada, in the late 1970s. Greg spent many days watching his brother, Mike, and another local pitching prospect, Mike Morgan, play baseball. Both were destined for the majors. Greg was soon following in their footsteps.

Greg was an all-state pitcher in his junior and senior seasons at Valley High School. He also played center field and was a member of the varsity basketball team. Valley coach Roger Fairless had earned a reputation for producing major-league prospects, and he thought Greg was something special.

Fairless remembers, "[Greg] threw in the mid-80s, maybe got it up to 86 miles an hour once in a while. We've had guys in the 90s, but the thing that always made Greg different was his control and poise on the mound.

"He just never got behind, never got in trouble, and his fastball always had good movement. He pitched the same no matter what team we were playing and what the score."

☆ ☆ ☆

Greg graduated from high school in 1984. The Chicago Cubs thought enough of him to make him their second choice in the '84 draft. Greg also had an offer to attend the University of Arizona on a baseball scholarship, but he chose to sign with the Cubs.

Greg moved quickly through the Cubs' minor-league system. He tied for the rookie-league lead in shutouts his first season, then won 13 games the next year at Class A Peoria. He moved up to AA in 1986, and pitched so well he was promoted to AAA Iowa. There, he won 10 of 11 decisions and tied again for the league lead in shutouts.

At this point, the Cubs knew that Greg had the potential to be a major-league star. But stardom rarely happens overnight. It would take Greg several more years of hard work before he became the Cubs' ace.

Greg (left) with teammates on the AAA Iowa Cubs

☆ ☆ ☆

The Cubs had won their division in 1984 with a veteran pitching staff, including Rick Sutcliffe, Dennis Eckersley, Scott Sanderson, and Steve Trout. But in the following years, those pitchers suffered a series of injuries. The Cubs needed help, and in September 1986, they called up Greg. At the age of 20, he was in the majors.

Greg made his debut in the 18th inning of a game against the Houston Astros, and gave up a homer to lose the game. But he got a start a few days later, against the Reds. The Reds' best player was Dave Parker, a big, left-handed hitter. Greg came inside with a hard fastball. Parker glared at him with a look that warned: rookies shouldn't pitch veterans that way. Greg came right back in with another tight fastball.

Dave Parker got to Greg for three hits that night, but he was the only hitter who did. Greg went the distance for an 11-3 victory—his first major-league win.

At age 20, Greg began his brilliant career at Wrigley Field in Chicago.

Greg's brother, Mike Maddux, pitched for several teams, including the Philadelphia Phillies.

☆ ☆ ☆

Greg had finally caught up with his brother, Mike. Both were rookie pitchers in 1986—Mike with the Philadelphia Phillies. They pitched against each other that September. It was the first time in major-league history that rookie brothers started the same game. Greg came out the winner, 8-3.

Greg had learned a lot from Mike. Many people said Mike helped Greg arrive in the majors as a mature adult rather than as an immature kid. Gordon Goldsberry, a Cubs executive, compared Greg's composure to another successful rookie, Robin Yount. "When Robin was in high school," said Goldsberry, "he had an older brother in the minors, and sometimes he'd go stay with him for a few weeks. In Greg's case, you could just see the professionalism coming through."

"It did really help, especially in the minors," recalls Greg. "Mike had been to every level of ball, and he gave me a lot of tips."

☆ ☆ ☆

Greg was still only 20 years old in the spring of 1987, but he made the Cubs' starting rotation. He was the youngest player in the majors. But his first full season wasn't easy. When he threw his curveball for strikes, he pitched well. But when he had trouble with his curve, he had to come in with his fastball. Big-league hitters were ready and ate up his fastball.

Late in the season, the Cubs sent Greg back to Iowa to work on his control. "It was a key time," says Dick Pole, who was then the Cubs' pitching coach. "He could've moped. He had 72 hours to report [to Iowa], but he was there the next day. He wanted to get to work on the things that would help." Greg won three of the four games he pitched at Iowa and came right back to the majors—this time for good.

By 1988, Greg had established himself as a solid major-league starting pitcher.

In 1988, the first night game in Wrigley Field history was delayed by rain. Greg and some of his teammates entertained the fans with belly flops on the rain-soaked tarp.

★ ★ ★

Greg and Mike went to Venezuela in the off-season to work with Pole in the winter leagues. By the time spring training rolled around, Greg was a mature pitcher. He and his father set a goal for him to win 12 games in 1988. Greg won 15—in the first half of the season alone! He was named to the National League All-Star team. "It's something I never thought of before," said Greg. "How could I when I was 6-14 last year?" At age 22, Greg was considered one of the best young pitchers in baseball.

Still, Greg struggled in the second half of the season. Some critics said he was tired from pitching winter ball, although Greg never used that excuse. He also got off to a slow start in 1989, losing five of his first six decisions. But he straightened himself out to get to 8-7 at the All-Star break. From then on, he was almost unbeatable.

☆ ☆ ☆

The rest of the Cubs caught Greg's winning attitude. Led by feisty manager Don Zimmer, the Cubs surprised the league with their gritty determination to win. On September 26, Greg beat the Montreal Expos 3-2 for his 19th victory. The win also clinched first place for the Cubs.

Greg could have gone for his 20th victory on the final weekend of the season, but he decided to rest up for the playoffs. The rest didn't pay off, however. Greg was hit hard by the San Francisco Giants in the first game. The Cubs won the second game to even the series, but then the two teams went to San Francisco, where the Giants won three straight to take the pennant. Greg didn't pitch much better in his second game. It was a depressing day for Greg and his teammates when the Giants eliminated the Cubs from the playoffs. On the flight back to Chicago, Greg tried to put his disappointing performance behind him. "I thought about it the four hours we had to get home, and that was that," he said. Greg was ready for new challenges.

Manager Don Zimmer (left) helped fire up the Cubs in 1989, and Greg's 19 victories led the team to the playoffs. But in his first post-season start, the Giants hammered Greg, and Zimmer had to take him out of the game (bottom). Greg would have to wait four years before he could redeem himself in the post-season.

Greg breathed a big sigh of relief after breaking his 1990 losing streak.

In 1990, things started well as Greg won four of his first five games. That gave him 49 career victories, but the 50th was a long time coming. He endured the worst slump of his career, going from May 5 until July 18 without a win. He lost eight games in a row! Scouts said he wasn't throwing as hard as before. They wondered if he was hurt or—even worse—washed up. Greg simply felt he wasn't making good pitches when he needed them.

After breaking out of the slump with a July win over the Padres, Greg reflected, "It's really the first time I've really struggled, where things haven't gone my way. It's been a while. Everybody knows that. I'm just glad to finally win. Maybe it will be the start of something good."

Was it ever! Greg won six of his next seven starts and finished 1990 with a 15-15 record. He won 15 again in 1991, but he pitched much more consistently. He had a newfound determination to make good pitches, and his control was better than ever.

Veteran pitcher Rick Sutcliffe was Greg's teammate on the Cubs and observed him through his slumps and his successes. Sutcliffe says that while most pitchers work "in and out," Greg learned to move the ball "up and down." "And when he keeps the ball down he's very tough. When he consistently throws the ball down he's had some of the easiest innings I've ever seen."

Rick Sutcliffe

Not only is Greg a great pitcher, he is a fine batter, fielder, and base runner.

Greg was now recognized as one of the best starters in the National League. To start 1992, he was given a $4-million, one-year contract. That made him the highest-paid Cub in history (until Ryne Sandberg signed a bigger contract later that year). But Greg's one-year contract would also make him a free agent at the end of the season. Throughout the season, people wondered if he would sign a long-term deal with the Cubs, or become a free agent and leave Chicago.

☆ ☆ ☆

Meanwhile, Greg went about his job as a professional and pitched the best baseball of his life. As the ace of a mediocre Cub team, Greg was 15-10 by late August. He then closed out the season by winning five of his last six decisions. He became the first Cub pitcher in 15 years to win 20 games. Amazingly, he was pitching in Wrigley Field, a park that favors hitters. Still, Greg finished with a sparkling 2.18 ERA.

Greg's teammates congratulate him after his 20th victory of 1992, a shutout of the Pirates. It turned out to be Greg's last game in a Cub uniform.

The nation's sportswriters named Greg the 1992 Cy Young Award winner as the best pitcher in the National League. When he accepted the award, Greg said he'd had two goals in his career: to win the Cy Young and to win the World Series. Now the rest of his career would be devoted to winning a championship.

The Cubs had finished fourth in three straight seasons, and it didn't seem likely that

In November 1992, Greg was overjoyed to receive his first Cy Young Award (above).

A month after winning the Cy Young Award, Greg changed teams by signing with the Atlanta Braves.

they'd improve very soon. So Greg, now a free agent, began listening to offers from other teams. The Yankees offered a lot more money than the Cubs, but Greg didn't want to move his family to New York City. When the Atlanta Braves topped the Cubs' offer, Greg leaped at the chance to sign with them. His five-year contract would pay him $28 million.

★ ★ ★

The Braves had been in the World Series two years in a row. They had lost both Series, but they had one of the most explosive lineups and the best pitching staff in baseball. The rotation included Tom Glavine, Steve Avery, and John Smoltz. Glavine had won the Cy Young Award in 1991, and Smoltz had led the league in strikeouts in 1992. By adding Greg Maddux to this group, the Braves had built the greatest rotation in decades.

Atlanta manager Bobby Cox chose Greg to open the season. Oddly enough, the Opening Day game was against his old teammates, the Cubs. Opposing Greg on the mound would be Mike Morgan, the pitcher he had looked up to when they were both teenagers in Las Vegas. Morgan remained one of Greg's best friends from the Cubs, and they still played golf together. Maddux and Morgan locked horns in a classic pitching duel, and Maddux's Braves won, 1-0. Greg, who is normally cool and controlled, said, "I had jitters for the whole game."

With the Braves, Greg was part of one of the greatest pitching staffs in history. Greg joined the outstanding young pitchers Steve Avery (top left), John Smoltz (top right), and Tom Glavine (bottom).

Greg and the Braves celebrate after beating the Cubs on Opening Day in 1993. Greg's performance set the pace for Atlanta's 104-win season.

☆ ☆ ☆

With that great start, both Greg and the Braves were off and running. Yet so were the San Francisco Giants. As well as the Braves played in 1993, they trailed the Giants all summer. By late September, the Braves were still alive and gaining on the Giants. On the second-to-last day of the season, Greg beat the Expos 10-1 for his 20th victory of the season. The next day, the Braves won again and the Giants lost, giving Atlanta first place. It was one of the most thrilling pennant drives in memory.

Atlanta went on to meet the Philadelphia Phillies in the playoffs. After the Phillies won Game One, Greg evened things up with a 14-3 victory in the second game. Back in 1989, Greg hadn't pitched well in the post-season. Now he had come through with a crucial playoff victory, proving he could win in the clutch.

But Greg's celebration was short-lived. By the time he got to pitch again, the Phils had taken a 3-2 series lead. Greg took the mound in a do-or-die Game Six matchup. In the first inning, Mickey Morandini lined a shot off Greg's right leg. Greg continued pitching, but he wasn't effective. The Phils got to him for two runs in the third, two more in the fifth, and another two in the sixth. The Braves' hitters couldn't rally, and Philadelphia went on to win the series. Atlanta's glorious season was over.

Greg refused to use the injury as an excuse for losing. He admitted he couldn't use his injured leg to push off the mound, but he said, "Your location gets better. Your velocity might go down a bit, but your location gets better."

After the post-season disappointment wore off, however, Greg was happy to be voted the National League Cy Young Award winner once again. Tom Glavine, Bill Swift, and John Burkett had each won more games than Greg, but Maddux had led the majors with a 2.36 ERA.

In 1994, Greg continued dominating National League hitters. By mid-August, he was rolling along with a 16-6 record and an astonishing 1.56 ERA. He was also tied for the league lead with

Atlanta

three shutouts, and he had thrown complete games 10 of the 25 times he started. But on August 12, Greg's brilliant season, and all of baseball, ground to a sudden, shocking halt. After months of conflict with the team owners, the baseball players were on strike. The strike wound up canceling the last six weeks of the regular season, as well as the playoffs and World Series. Although Greg was enjoying the best season of his career, he did not hesitate to join his fellow players on strike. He believed it was the right thing to do.

The shortened season did not stop Greg from gaining recognition in the post-season awards. In October 1994, Greg was again voted the National League's Cy Young Award winner. He had become the first pitcher in history to win the award three years in a row. Only five other pitchers had won as many as three Cy Young awards.

At age 28, Greg was at the top of his skills, and he had risen to the top of the baseball world. Now there was no doubt that Greg Maddux was the finest pitcher of his generation.

☆ ☆ ☆

Chronology

1966 – April 14: Gregory Alan Maddux is born to Dave and Linda Maddux.

1984 – Greg graduates from high school and is drafted in the second round by the Chicago Cubs. He begins his professional career with the Pikeville team in the Appalachian League.

1986 – Greg moves from AA (Pittsfield), to AAA (Iowa), to the major leagues in one season. In 18 games with the AAA Iowa Cubs, he compiles a 10-1 record.
– In September, Greg makes his major-league debut.

1987 – Greg has a rough rookie season, going 6-14 with a 5.61 ERA. He goes to AAA Iowa for a brief stint and scores a 3-0 record with a brilliant 0.98 ERA.

1988 – Greg establishes himself as the ace of the Cubs' pitching staff with an 18-8 record and a 3.18 ERA.

1989 – Greg wins 19 games and leads the Chicago Cubs to the National League's Eastern Division crown. In the NL Championship Series, Greg is blown out in his two starts against the San Francisco Giants. Greg goes 0-1 with a 13.50 ERA in the series. The Cubs are eliminated by the San Francisco Giants.

☆ ☆ ☆

1992 – Greg wins 20 games for the first time in his career and wins the National League Cy Young Award. He is the first Cub pitcher to capture the award since Rick Sutcliffe, in 1984. He also wins his third consecutive Gold Glove as the best defensive pitcher in the National League.

– October 26: Greg files for free agency.

– December 9: Greg signs five-year contract with the Atlanta Braves.

1993 – Greg wins 20 games for the second straight year, leads the NL in innings pitched for the third straight year, and captures his second Cy Young Award in a row. He is the first back-to-back Cy Young winner since Roger Clemens, in 1986–87.

– Greg wins Game Two of the NL Championship Series, but is injured and pitches poorly in Game Six. He goes 1-1 with a 4.97 ERA in the series. The Braves are eliminated by the Philadelphia Phillies.

1994 – Greg posts a league-best 16-6 record and a 1.56 ERA in a strike-shortened season. He is the first pitcher in history to win three consecutive Cy Young Awards.

Gregory Alan Maddux

Date of Birth: April 14, 1966
Place of Birth: San Angelo, Texas
Height: 6 feet
Weight: 175 pounds
Home: Las Vegas, Nevada
Pro Teams: Chicago Cubs, Atlanta Braves
Won NL Cy Young Award: 1992, 1993, 1994

MAJOR–LEAGUE STATISTICS

Season	Team	Wins	Losses	ERA	Strikeouts	Walks
1986	Chicago (NL)	2	4	5.52	20	11
1987	Chicago (NL)	6	14	5.61	101	74
1988	Chicago (NL)	18	8	3.18	140	81
1989	Chicago (NL)	19	12	2.95	135	82
1990	Chicago (NL)	15	15	3.46	144	71
1991	Chicago (NL)	15	11	3.35	198	66
1992	Chicago (NL)	**20**	11	2.18	199	70
1993	Atlanta	20	10	**2.36**	197	52
1994*	Atlanta	**16**	6	**1.56**	140	70
Totals (9 Seasons)		131	91	3.01	1,274	577

(**Boldface** indicates led league)
*The 1994 season was shortened by a players' strike.

☆ ☆ ☆

About the Author

Ted Cox is a Chicago journalist who works at the *Daily Southtown*. He has covered sports for the *Chicago Reader* and *Chicago* magazine, and has worked at United Press International. Ted is the author of several other titles in the Childrens Press *Sports Stars* series, including *Mario Lemieux*, *Shaquille O'Neal*, *Emmitt Smith*, and *Frank Thomas*. He holds a B.S. in journalism from the University of Illinois at Urbana-Champaign. He lives in Chicago with his wife, Catherine, and their daughter, Sadie.